HARRY POTTER

The Complete Quiz Book

Unofficial & Unauthorised

Jack Goldstein & Frankie Taylor

Published in 2014 by
AUK Authors, an imprint of
Andrews UK Limited
www.andrewsuk.com

Contents

The Questions

The Answers

Introduction

How much do you know about the world of Harry Potter, his friends and of course his enemies? Do you know what language Merpeople speak? How long does felix felicis take to prepare? Who played Delores Umbridge in the films? And what colour hue does the Dogbreath potion have?

This fantastically fun quiz book contains eight hundred questions (and answers!) covering every aspect of wizarding life including the characters, life at Hogwarts, spells, potions, fantastic beasts plus much, much more. It contains all of the questions from both Jack Goldstein's *Ultimate Quiz Book* and Frankie Taylor's *Amazing Quiz Book*, even adding some completely new ones!

From questions even a muggle could answer all the way through to trivia that would test Dumbledore himself, this is the perfect way to test your Harry Potter knowledge

Good luck with the quiz!

Jack & Frankie
April 2014

HARRY POTTER
The Complete Quiz Book

The Questions

Harry - Part 1

1. When is Harry's birthday?

2. Where does Harry live?

3. Who brought Harry to the Dursley household as a baby?

4. What is the shape of the Harry's prominent scar?

5. What animal did Harry talk to at the zoo?

6. What was Harry's father's first name?

7. ...and his mother's?

8. What special gift did Harry get on his first Christmas morning at Hogwarts?

9. What animal is produced by Harry's Patronus spell?

10. Who did Harry share his first kiss with?

Spells – Part 1

What do these spells do?

11. Reparo

12. Accio

13. Engorgio

14. Expelliarmus

15. Riddikulus

16. Incendio

17. Lumos

18. Sonorus

19. Confundo

20. Muffliato

21. What is Hermione's middle name?

22. What animal is Hermione's Patronus?

23. With whom does Hermione attend the Yule Ball?

24. Into which house is Hermione sorted?

25. What is the name of Hermione's pet cat?

26. What effect did the densaugeo spell have on Hermione?

27. In which subject did Hermione not get an outstanding grade O.W.L.?

28. What spell does Hermione use on Neville in the first book?

29. What profession are both Hermione's parents?

30. In which month is Hermione's birthday?

Who Plays - Part 1

In the films, who plays these characters?

31. Harry Potter

32. Rubeus Hagrid

33. Uncle Vernon Dursley

34. Ginny Weasley

35. Ron Weasley

36. Hermione Granger

37. Draco Malfoy

38. Nearly Headless Nick

39. Severus Snape

40. Sirius Black

Ron – Part 1

41. What colour is Ron's hair?

42. What is Ron's middle name?

43. How many siblings does Ron have?

44. What does Ron get from his mum after using the flying car to get to school?

45. What did Ron buy Harry for his 13th birthday?

46. What did Ron try to repair his wand with?

47. Which character does Ron play in the game of chess in the first book?

48. True or false: Ron is pure-blood?

49. Which animal is Ron most scared of?

50. What quidditch position does Ron play?

51. Which Gryffindor girl did Ron date for a short time, once receiving a *My Sweetheart* necklace from her?

52. What was the occupation of the Creeveys' father?

53. What position does Fay Dunbar play at quidditch?

54. What form does Seamus's Patronus take?

55. Who does Angelina Johnson attend the Yule Ball with?

56. What is Neville's toad called?

57. Why could Cormac McLaggen not take part in quidditch trials in his sixth year?

58. Who gives Harry a love-potion-laced box of Chocolate Cauldrons?

59. Which Gryffindor student hosts Potterwatch?

60. What was in the note from Professor Snape that Demelza Robbins brought to Harry?

61. What does the Hogwarts motto *Draco Dormiens Nunquam Titillandus* mean?

62. What object decides which houses the students will go into?

63. What colour is the Slytherin banner?

64. Who – or what – is Peeves?

65. What are the creatures that pull the Hogwarts carriages called?

66. What is the password to the Gryffindor common room in Harry's first year?

67. Which four animals are on the Hogwarts coat of arms?

68. In Harry's first year at Hogwarts, whose name is the first to be called out for sorting?

69. How many items are there on Filch's list of forbidden objects?

70. What is the password to open the prefects' bathroom?

71. Name Filch's cat.

72. Which centaur becomes the Hogwarts divination teacher?

73. What does madame Pomfrey use to heal Harry's arm after Gilderoy Lockhart has made a real mess of it?

74. What is the full name of the professor who has Voldemort's head under his turban?

75. Who is the astronomy teacher at Hogwarts during Harry's time there?

76. Name one of Snape's nicknames.

77. Which house is Professor Sprout head of?

78. Who sacked Professor Trelawney?

79. What was the name of the muggle studies teacher who was killed by Voldemort?

80. Who took over from Hagrid as the teacher for care of magical creatures?

81. What are the three different forms of wizarding currency?

82. Who guards the wizarding prison of Azkaban?

83. What is the name of the wizard's hospital?

84. Who greets you at reception there?

85. ...and who founded it?

86. What is the name of the wizard high court of law?

87. Name the main wizarding newspaper.

88. What is the name of the all-wizard village children can visit (with permission from their parents)?

89. ...and what do the Harry, Ron and Hermione buy to drink there?

90. From what material is a remembrall made?

Fantastic Beasts - Part 1

Can you name the creature being described?

91. A species of giant spider native to the rainforests of Southeastern Asia.

92. Has the head and torso of a human on the lower body of a horse.

93. Often referred to as the 'biting fairy', venom used for skiving snackboxes.

94. Toothless brown worm that eats cabbage and lettuce.

95. Has the front legs, wings and head of a giant eagle, and the hindquarters of a horse.

96. Magical feline similar to a large housecat.

97. Mischievous magical prankster native to Ireland.

98. Infests mistletoe – according to Luna Lovegood.

99. Large scarlet-coloured bird which can be reborn from its ashes.

100. Skeletal horse only visible to those who have witnessed death.

Creatures and Animals - Part 1

101. What is Fluffy guarding in the first book?

102. ...and what puts him to sleep?

103. What is the name of Neville's toad?

104. What is the name of the Weasley family's owl?

105. What is the hippogriff Harry meets in his third year called?

106. ...and when he is given a new name, what is it?

107. What sort of dog is Fang?

108. What creature is hiding in the Chamber of Secrets?

109. The blood of which creature kept Lord Voldemort alive in the first book?

110. ...and at what age does this creature grow its horns?

111. What bird does Professor Dumbledore keep as a pet?

112. ...and what is its name?

113. What does it bring Harry in the Chamber of Secrets?

114. What mysterious dark magical items are Harry and Dumbledore trying to find in the latter books?

115. ...and how many does Dumbledore believe there are?

116. Where does Dumbledore store his excess memories?

117. Which wizard did Dumbledore defeat in 1945?

118. What stuffed creature was atop the witch's hat that came out of the cracker Dumbledore and Snape pulled?

119. Professor Dumbledore has a scar above his left knee in the shape of what?

120. How many uses of dragon blood did Dumbledore discover?

121. What is Sirius's nickname?

122. How many years did he spend in Azkaban?

123. Who eventually killed Sirius?

124. ...and what relationship were they to him?

125. How did Sirius escape from Azkaban?

126. What did Sirius give to Hagrid at the time of James and Lily Potter's death?

127. What is the address of the house that Sirius bequeaths to Harry?

128. ...and who is the house elf who lives there?

129. What was the name of Sirius's younger brother?

130. What nickname do Harry, Ron and Hermione give to Sirius so they can talk about him in public?

131. What are the three balls used in quidditch called?

132. How many points is it worth to catch the smallest ball?

133. How many players are in a quidditch team?

134. What are the playing positions in quidditch?

135. Who are Ron's favourite quidditch team?

136. What type of broomstick is Harry given in the first book?

137. Who is captain of the Gryffindor quidditch team when Harry joins Hogwarts?

138. Who was responsible for the rogue bludger in the second book?

139. Who was the captain of Slytherin's quidditch team in Harry's first year?

140. How many quidditch fouls are there?

141. What did Malfoy take that belonged to Neville in their first year at Hogwarts?

142. What is Crabbe's first name?

143. What offensive term did Malfoy first call Hermione in their second year?

144. Which shop does Draco attend in Knockturn Alley?

145. Which two Hogwarts employees does Harry ask to watch Malfoy together?

146. How are Crabbe and Goyle disguised when on look out?

147. Who did Draco take to the yule ball?

148. To what size did Draco's nose swell during one of Professor Snape's potions classes?

149. Who dressed up as dementors to scare Harry, along with Malfoy, Crabbe and Goyle?

150. Which spell did Professor Snape suggest Draco cast on Harry at the duelling club?

Spells - Part 2

What would you say if you wanted to cast the following spells?

151. The killing curse.

152. This opens or unlocks doors.

153. Turns an object into a portkey.

154. Silences the target immediately.

155. Conjures a Patronus.

156. Inflicts unbearable pain on the target.

157. Renders the victim unconscious.

158. Reveals the last spell cast by a wand.

159. Removes memories of an event from the target.

160. Conjures the dark mark.

161. Where can you find Harry's prominent scar?

162. Who attended Harry's christening?

163. Into which other house did the sorting hat consider putting Harry?

164. What is Harry's middle name?

165. Which birthday was Harry (not) celebrating when he found out he was a Wizard?

166. Harry is the only known survivor of which curse?

167. What was Harry's first broomstick whilst at Hogwarts?

168. Name Harry's muggle aunt and uncle.

169. Who does Harry eventually marry at the end of the series?

170. Harry's aunt and uncle had always led him to believe that his parents had died in which way?

Patronuses

Can you name the animal form of the Patronus of these characters?

171. Harry Potter

172. Ron Weasley

173. Ginny Weasley

174. Albus Dumbledore

175. Kingsley Shacklebolt

176. Luna Lovegood

177. Severus Snape

178. Dolores Umbridge

179. Cho Chang

180. Aberforth Dumbledore

181. What is the name for the language used when talking to snakes?

182. What ability do you have if you are an animagus?

183. What potion reverses the effect of the draught of living death?

184. The hair from which animal is used to make invisibility cloaks?

185. What happens over time however?

186. What power does a legilimens have?

187. ...and an occlumens?

188. What potion eases the symptoms of lycanthropy?

189. What is a mandrake also known as?

190. What does Baruffio's Brain Elixir do to you?

The Weasleys - Part 1

191. What is Ron's full name?

192. What does Ron's boggart transform into?

193. Name all of Ron's brothers and sisters.

194. In the final story, one of the twins loses his life during the battle at Hogwarts – but which twin is it?

195. Who or what is Errol?

196. Ginny took possession of a diary which forced her to open something that endangered the life of many students. What did she open?

197. What is the (animal) name of Ron's pet rat?

198. Charlie Weasley graduated from Hogwarts and studied dragons in which country?

199. During the battle at the astronomy tower, Bill was attacked by which creature?

200. What is make of the car which Ron flies Harry to Hogwarts in one year?

Other Characters – Part 1

201. Who is the headmaster at Hogwarts in Harry's first year?

202. What are *He Who Must Not Be Named*'s trusted supporters called?

203. Who runs The Three Broomsticks?

204. Who is the conductor on the Knight Bus?

205. ...and who is the driver?

206. Who was the creator of the Philosopher's Stone?

207. Who is the main commentator at Hogwarts for the quidditch matches?

208. What's the name of Colin Creevey's brother?

209. What is the name of Sirius Black's younger brother?

210. Who was killed by a forbidden curse instead of Harry at the end of his fourth year?

211. How did the Bloody Baron die?

212. With which Slytherin student does Hermione physically fight in duelling club?

213. What positions do Crabbe and Goyle play in quidditch?

214. What spell does Crabbe cast which leads to his and Goyle's death?

215. For how many years did Marcus Flint study at Hogwarts?

216. During their first flying lesson, who teases Parvati Patil for defending Neville when his remembrall is stolen by Malfoy?

217. During Slughorn's lunch on the Hogwarts Express, which Slytherin student tells of how his mother was left pots of galleons from her many husbands, all of whom died suspicious deaths?

218. Apart from Harry and Neville, who else can see the thestrals in Hagrid's care of magical creatures class?

219. Who was captain of the Slytherin quidditch team from Harry's third year onwards?

220. Who is Slytherin's seeker before Draco Malfoy is given the job?

Books and the Like - Part 1

221. What colour are howlers?

222. Rita Skeeter is a reporter for which newspaper?

223. Where did Hermione read about the ceiling at Hogwarts?

224. ...and who wrote it?

225. What must you do to the *Monster Book of Monsters* to open it?

226. Which magazine test rides all new broomsticks?

227. What is the name of the best-selling wizard magazine?

228. What award did *Witch Weekly* give Gilderoy Lockhart?

229. Who wrote *A History of Magic*?

230. Harry borrowed a copy of *Advanced Potion Making*; who did it belong to previously?

The Weasleys - Part 2

231. What are Mr & Mrs Weasley's first names?

232. Which of the Weasleys is taken into the Chamber of Secrets?

233. What is the make and model of the flying car?

234. What is the name of the house where the Weasleys live?

235. How many hands does the Weasley family's clock have?

236. Who does Ginny date before Harry?

237. What do Fred and George use to listen into conversations?

238. Which member of the Weasley family has a pony-tail and an earring?

239. ...and who is he engaged to?

240. In which department was Mr Weasley found after being attacked?

241. Which girl did Cedric invite to the Yule Ball before Harry could pluck up the courage?

242. Which Ravenclaw student during Harry's time at Hogwarts had an uncle by the name of Damocles?

243. What potion does Eddie Carmichael claim helped him achieve nine 'outstandings' in his O.W.L. exams?

244. Name Percy Weasley's Ravenclaw girlfriend from his Hogwarts years.

245. Name the ghost who haunts the first-floor girls' bathroom.

246. Parvati Patil is sorted into Gryffindor, but who is her twin who is placed into Ravenclaw?

247. Helena Ravenclaw is Ravenclaw's house ghost – but what is she better known as?

248. When Harry first attends Hogwarts, which teacher is head of Ravenclaw house?

249. Which Ravenclaw student was Fleur Delacour's date at the Yule Ball?

250. Apart from Harry, who dates both Ginny Weasley and Cho Chang?

251. Who teaches charms?

252. Who teaches transfiguration?

253. ...and how long has he or she been at Hogwarts?

254. What animal can he or she turn into?

255. Who teaches history of magic?

256. What is Professor Lupin's secret?

257. What is Professor Sprout's first name?

258. Who was headmaster when Tom Riddle was at Hogwarts?

259. Who taught care of magical creatures before Hagrid?

260. What secret did Harry discover about Filch which might explain his grumpy demeanour?

261. Which plant likes to wrap itself around its victims?

262. What language do Merpeople speak?

263. To which local comprehensive school was Harry due to go?

264. How did Sirius Black escape from prison?

265. ...and what name do the trio refer to him as?

266. What part of you is hidden in a horcrux?

267. Which sickly-sweet (by appearance, anyway!) teacher became the new defence against the dark arts teacher in the fifth book?

268. Which family did Dobby serve?

269. What colour is the knight bus?

270. In which English county does Nicolas Flamel live?

Teachers and Their Subjects

Which subject do the following professors teach?

271. Professor Babbling

272. Professor Burbage

273. Professor Binns

274. Professor Flitwick

275. Professor Slughorn

276. Professor McGonagall

277. Professor Sprout

278. Madame Hooch

279. Professor Vector

280. Professor Trelawney

Hermione - Part 2

281. In Hermione's second year, why didn't the letters she wrote to Harry during the holidays reach him?

282. Which musical instrument can Hermione play well?

283. Who does Slughorn think Hermione might be related to?

284. Where did Hermione first meet Harry?

285. Which creature once petrified Hermione?

286. What word does Hermione have barbarically carved into her arm?

287. Name the object that allowed Hermione to attend more classes than the other students thought possible.

288. ...and who sent it to her?

289. After which year did Hermione leave Hogwarts?

290. What form did Hermione's boggart take?

Shops

291. Where did Harry buy his wand?

292. How many galleons did it cost?

293. Who owns the ice cream parlour in Diagon Alley?

294. What are the names of the two pubs in Hogsmeade?

295. What is the name of Fred and George's business in the later books?

296. ...and what is its address?

297. What does Madam Malkin sell?

298. What is the name of the main sweet shop in Hogsmeade?

299. Where would you go in Diagon Alley to buy a pet?

300. How much does it cost for a course of apparition lessons?

301. What is His name (after he changed it)?

302. What is the name of His snake?

303. True or false: He is pure-blood?

304. How many brothers did He have?

305. What is the length of His wand?

306. Who paid for Him to attend Hogwarts?

307. Who did He go to work for when he left Hogwarts?

308. How much did His mother sell a particular locket for?

309. What three things do He and Harry have in common?

310. What is the name of the village where the Riddles lived?

Hagrid

311. What did Hagrid give Harry for Christmas in the first book?

312. ...and what was his official job title at the time?

313. Where does Hagrid keep his wand?

314. What was the name of Hagrid's dragon?

315. ...and what type of dragon is he?

316. What did Hagrid give to Harry for his thirteenth birthday?

317. Who does Hagrid believe is also a half-giant?

318. Which of Hagrid's parents was a giant?

319. ...and what was he or she called?

320. What is the name of the giant that Hagrid brings back with him from a trip away from Hogwarts?

Dobby

321. Which family did Dobby serve before being freed?

322. What unusual punishment did Dobby once inflict on his hands?

323. How much was Dobby paid per week for working in the kitchens at Hogwarts?

324. When Dobby rescues his friends from Malfoy Manor, under whose orders is he working?

325. Where is Dobby's grave?

326. Which quidditch ball does Dobby enchant during a match?

327. Name the female elf who Dobby looks after when she is freed.

328. How did Dobby come across the room of requirement?

329. What does Dobby name Ron?

330. What are Dobby's final words?

Ron - Part 2

331. Who does Ron ask for an autograph in the fourth book?

332. When Ron gets a new wand in the third book, what is it made of?

333. ...and how long was it?

334. Who gave Pigwidgeon to Ron following the loss of Scabbers?

335. ...and who actually named it?

336. What does Dumbledore bequeath Ron in his will?

337. What did Harry buy Ron for his 17th birthday?

338. What did Ron eat that contained a love potion?

339. On the subject of girls, who did Ron date, kiss and break up with?

340. When Ron was poisoned what did Harry use to save him?

341. To whom is the only person Harry has ever given an autograph?

342. How old (in years and months) was Harry when Voldemort tried to murder him?

343. During a tea leaf reading in divination, what shape appeared in the bottom of Harry's cup?

344. Who first shows Harry the diary of Tom Riddle?

345. When Harry let the boa constrictor out during his trip to the zoo, where did it plan on going?

346. When Harry first met Oliver Wood on the Quidditch pitch, he compared the game to which muggle sport?

347. Name the school that Harry was instructed to tell aunt Marge he attended.

348. Which type of dragon was Harry pitted against in his triwizard task?

349. Harry and Voldemort's wands share the same core; what is it?

350. What did Dumbledore leave to Harry in his will?

351. Who haunts the girls' toilets on the first floor?

352. How many secret passages lead from Hogwarts to Hogsmeade?

353. Who usually guards the entrance to the Gryffindor Tower?

354. What are O.W.L.s?

355. What is the place that the DA practice in called?

356. How many schools take part in the Triwizard Tournament?

357. Name them!

358. ...and what is now the minimum age for a competitor?

359. What does the flying car crash into at Hogwarts?

360. What was Quirrell trying to get out of the mirror in the first book?

Who Said?

Name the character who said each of the following quotes:

361. "Alas, earwax!"

362. "You're a wizard, Harry."

363. "Why couldn't it be 'follow the butterflies'?"

364. "I shudder to think what the state of my in-tray would be if I was away from work for five days."

365. "You may not like him, Minister, but you can't deny: Dumbledore's got style."

366. "You are the most insensitive wart I have ever had the misfortune to meet."

367. "Reading? Hmm. I didn't know you could read."

368. "I can make bad things happen to people who are mean to me."

369. "You're the weak one. And you'll never know love, or friendship. And I feel sorry for you."

370. "But know this; the ones that love us never really leave us. And you can always find them in here."

371. What got into the castle on Halloween night of Harry's first term?

372. What type of owl is Hedwig?

373. What kind of creature is Aragog?

374. ...and who attended his funeral?

375. What did Professor Slughorn want from Aragog's body?

376. Where is Kreacher sent to work?

377. Name the centaur who helped Harry in the forbidden forest.

378. Which animal represents 'The Grim'?

379. What is Sirius's house-elf called?

380. On what does Professor Moody demonstrate the Imperius Curse?

381. Who was the only girl on the Ravenclaw quidditch team?

382. Who insists that Harry and his friends support the Ireland quidditch team at the world cup?

383. ...and who did Ireland beat in the semi-final?

384. Who did they play in the final?

385. ...and which of these two won?

386. Who refereed the final?

387. How much were a pair of omnioculars at the world cup?

388. Which type of wood is the handle of a Nimbus 2000 made from?

389. Who banned Harry from playing quidditch in his fifth year?

390. What make of broom does Harry get in his third year?

Who Plays - Part 2

In the films, who plays these characters?

391. Professor Minerva McGonagall

392. Professor Quirinus Quirrell

393. Molly Weasley

394. Fred & George Weasley

395. Neville Longbottom

396. Vincent Crabbe

397. Gregory Goyle

398. Madame Hooch

399. Lucius Malfoy

400. Professor Gilderoy Lockhart

Hermione - Part 3

401. When Harry and Ron first met Hermione, they didn't seem to like her – she came across as a know-it-all. What single act however changed their perspective of her?

402. What are the initials of the society Hermione founded which concerns itself with rights for House elves?

403. The treatment of which house elf – and by whom – caused her to set it up?

404. What is the name of Hermione's two children at the end of the series?

405. Which other house did the sorting hat consider putting Hermione in?

406. ...and why?

407. Whose hair did Hermione think she had which actually turned out to be their cat's?

408. What form does Hermione's Patronus take?

409. What was Hermione left in Dumbledore's will?

410. What is the name of the charm that Hermione uses to enchant the coins for Dumbledore's Army?

Hufflepuffs

411. Name Hufflepuff's Triwizard champion.

412. Which Hufflepuff student firmly held a belief that Sirius Black could transform into a flowering shrub?

413. When Harry first attends Hogwarts, which teacher is head of Hufflepuff house?

414. Which Hufflepuff student asks Harry if he really can produce a fully corporeal patronus?

415. Who had his name down for posh Eton school before finding out that he could attend Hogwarts?

416. Who gave Harry a public apology after wrongly believing he was responsible for petrifying students during the *Chamber of Secrets* saga?

417. What is the name of Hufflepuff's house ghost?

418. Who laughs at Harry's choice to teach the supposedly simple spell *expelliarmus* to Dumbledore's Army?

419. Who succeeds Cedric Diggory as Hufflepuff's seeker?

420. When she is commentating on the quidditch match, whose name does Luna Lovegood forget, referring to him as 'Bibble or Buggins'?

421. What is the potion made from the Philosopher's stone called?

422. Harry, Ron and Hermione make which difficult potion in the second book to fool Malfoy?

423. What is mandrake root used for?

424. Which potion does Professor Lupin take regularly?

425. What is felix felicis?

426. ...and how long does it take to prepare?

427. Which plant did Harry use during one of the Triwizard challenges?

428. What happens when someone takes the potion veritaserum?

429. The pus from which plant is a powerful cure for acne?

430. ...and what does that plant look like?

Anagrams - Part 1

These are the names of Harry Potter characters, but the letters are jumbled up. Can you unscramble them?

431. Trophy Rater

432. Slick Airbus

433. Fly Cod Aroma

434. Go Valued Loon

435. A Bulbous Meddler

436. Nose Lawyer

437. Amusing Fannies

438. Enrage Grim Heron

439. Bushier Guard

440. Melon Bottle Loving

441. Where was Professor Binns when he died?

442. Which teacher conducts the school choir?

443. What is Madam Hooch's first name?

444. Who does Hagrid replace as the teacher for care of magical creatures?

445. What is Gilderoy Lockhart's favourite colour?

446. What creature was in the paddling pool Professor Lupin used for the third year students' end-of-year obstacle course test?

447. Name the spell Professor McGonagall uses to animate the warriors of Hogwarts.

448. Which village is Professor Slughorn hiding in when Dumbledore and Harry find him?

449. What law did Umbridge once propose about Merpeople?

450. Who was the caretaker at Hogwarts when Mr and Mrs Weasley attended?

Other Characters – Part 2

451. Which animal can Rita Skeeter turn into?

452. What is Fleur Delacour's sister called?

453. Who does Tonks fall in love with?

454. Who edits *The Quibbler*?

455. Who is the landlord of the Leaky Cauldron?

456. What does Nearly Headless Nick celebrate each year to which Harry and his friends are once invited?

457. Into which Hogwarts house was Owen Cauldwell sorted?

458. What are the first names of Sirius's evil cousins?

459. Who replaced Cornelius Fudge as Minister of Magic?

460. Who accidentally opens a parcel with a cursed necklace in it?

461. What two other names is the elder wand known by?

462. True or False: the word 'muggle' is now listed in the Oxford English Dictionary.

463. Name the three unforgiveable curses.

464. Who founded the original Order of the Phoenix?

465. What is the name of the luck potion which Professor Slughorn brews?

466. In *The Half Blood Prince,* we're told the entrance to the headmaster's office is located on which floor?

467. ...and what statue conceals it?

468. Name the conductor of the Knight Bus?

469. Name Hagrid's brother.

470. With its streamlined, super-fine handle of ash and hand-numbered with its own registration number, just *how* fast are we told the Firebolt broomstick accelerates?

Spells - Part 3

For the first five questions, what do these spells do?

For the second five, what would you say if you wanted to cast them?

471. Aguamenti

472. Incarcerous

473. Glisseo

474. Tarantallegra

475. Diffindo

476. Causes birds to attack a target.

477. Reveals nearby humans.

478. Causes the target's teeth to grow at an alarming rate.

479. The target feels like they're being tickled.

480. Makes things lower.

The Weasleys - Part 3

481. What magical item do the Weasley twins give to Harry in his third year?

482. What is Mr Weasley's nickname for his wife?

483. How many galleons was Mr Weasley fined for bewitching a car?

484. What does Mrs Weasley give Harry for supper when he arrives at the Burrow before starting his sixth year at Hogwarts?

485. Who is Percy Weasley's boss?

486. ...and what does he call Percy?

487. How many O.W.L.s did Percy take?

488. What is the name of Percy's (actual) owl?

489. What department is Mr Weasley the head of?

490. How many galleons were in the Weasleys' vault at Gringotts?

The Dursleys

491. What is the name of Uncle Vernon's company?

492. How many presents did Dudley get for his birthday in the first book?

493. What do Dudley's gang call him?

494. ...and what does Aunt Petunia call him?

495. What school do the Dursleys say Harry goes to?

496. How many dogs does Aunt Marge have in total?

497. ...and which department was sent to deflate her?

498. What colour were the tailcoats worn at Smeltings School?

499. Which one of the Dursleys throws ornaments at Mr Weasley?

500. To which hotel did Uncle Vernon take his family and Harry to escape Harry's initial letters from Hogwarts?

501. What is Professor Flitwick's first name?

502. What role does Professor Tofty have?

503. Which potions teacher returns to Hogwarts after a long absence?

504. Professor Grubby-Plank took over from which teacher?

505. Who is the new divination professor in Harry's final years?

506. What is Madame Pomfrey's first name?

507. Which dashing wizard becomes the defence against the dark arts teacher in Harry's second year?

508. Who is the head of Hufflepuff House?

509. Professor Sinistra teaches in which department at Hogwarts?

510. Who brought Colin Creevey to Madam Pomfrey?

511. What are N.E.W.T.s?

512. To where does the tunnel under the whomping willow lead?

513. Professor Trelawney's prophecy could apply to who else?

514. Who are Moony, Wormtail, Padfoot and Prongs better known as (make sure you get the correct order)?

515. Which member of the Order of the Phoenix is working for the muggle prime minister?

516. Who comes to Harry's rescue when he's hiding from Professor Lupin (in werewolf form)?

517. Which competitor wants to return to England to improve her language skills?

518. From which vault did Hagrid take something from at Gringotts?

519. What is the Gryffindor ghost's full name.

520. ...and how many times was he hit in the neck with a blunt axe?

521. What is Goyle's first name?

522. Malfoy was put on detention with Hagrid for being out past curfew and referred to his punishment as 'servant's stuff'. What were they looking for?

523. When Draco is assigned to kill Dumbledore, he becomes stressed leading him to confide in which mudblood?

524. Draco witnessed the murder of which Hogwarts teacher?

525. What core does Draco's wand have?

526. What are Draco Malfoy's parents called?

527. True or False: the Malfoy's are supposedly a family of pure-bloods.

528. Before Narcissa's marriage to Lucius Malfoy, what was her surname?

529. Which animal attacks Malfoy causing him to 'nearly lose his arm'?

530. Which animal is Draco turned into by the 'fake' Professor Moody?

531. Which book does Dumbledore bequeath to Hermione?

532. How many galleons formed the prize money in the *Daily Prophet's* 'prize galleon draw'?

533. What did Harry use to keep the *Monster Book of Monsters* shut?

534. What name got inscribed on Ron's *Advanced Potion Making* Book?

535. Who is the book's author?

536. Who wants to write Harry Potter's biography?

537. How did people who had read *Sonnets of a Sorcerer* speak for the rest of their lives?

538. In which book can you read about curse scars?

539. Who wrote *Curses and Counter Curses*?

540. Who wrote *The Dream Oracle*?

541. Aside from catching the snitch, how can a quidditch match be ended?

542. How many points is a goal worth?

543. ...and how many for catching the Snitch?

544. True or false: the quidditch world cup happens every five years?

545. What is bumphing?

546. When was the last time that all of the quidditch fouls were committed in one match?

547. Name any of the quidditch teams from the continent of Africa.

548. True or false: players may not take wands onto the pitch?

549. Name the only quidditch team we know of from Peru.

550. Who is the author of the book *Quidditch Through the Ages*?

551. What was the number of Harry's room at the Leaky Cauldron?

552. What interesting item did Harry find after his night visit to the library the first Christmas that he was at Hogwarts?

553. Who did Harry meet in the Leaky Cauldron before the start of his first year at Hogwarts?

554. Who looked after Harry when the Dursleys went out?

555. What was Harry's mother's maiden name?

556. What creature's feathers do Harry and Lord Voldemort have as part of their wands?

557. What does the scar on the back of Harry's hand say?

558. Which wood is Harry's wand made of?

559. Which wood was his father's wand made from?

560. Which career does Harry want to have?

561. What has a cockroach cluster got to do with Dumbledore?

562. Which house did the sorting hat place Albus Dumbledore in during his time as a student at Hogwarts?

563. What is the one use of dragon blood that Dumbledore tells Harry about?

564. What position was Dumbledore repeatedly offered but never accepted?

565. Dumbledore is pushed from the astronomy tower by whom?

566. What is the names of Dumbledore's brother?

567. ...and his sister?

568. Which member of Dumbledore's family was placed in Azkaban for attacking Muggles?

569. Aberforth Dumbledore was the owner of which pub?

570. What colour was Dumbledore's beard as a young wizard?

Who Plays - Part 3

In the films, who plays these characters?

571. Colin Creevey

572. Arthur Weasley

573. Professor Sybil Trelawney

574. Peter Pettigrew

575. Barty Crouch Junior

576. Cedric Diggory

577. Cho Chang

578. Fleur Delacour

579. Lord Voldemort

580. Rufus Scrimgeour

581. What does S.P.E.W. stand for?

582. ...and how much does it cost to join?

583. What did Hermione knit in relation to this?

584. On the subject of abbreviations, what does DA stand for?

585. ...and what does Hermione give to every member?

586. What spell did Hermione cast on a student during the quidditch trials?

587. ...and on whom did she cast it?

588. Whose party did she then take him to?

589. What exam clashes with Hermione's ancient runes one?

590. Who is Hermione married to at the end of the final book?

591. How old are witches and wizards when they come of age?

592. What are the four different types of blood purity?

593. What is the main lift at the Ministry of Magic disguised as?

594. What are dark wizard catchers called?

595. What is the name of the place in London where witches and wizards go to shop?

596. Which object is used to transport wizards from one place to another at an arranged time?

597. How long ago was the Triwizard Tournament started?

598. How many people have survived the Avada Kedavra curse?

599. What is the address of Sirius's house?

600. What is the name of the department store which hides the main wizarding hospital?

601. What job are we told in the early books that Snape really wants?

602. Where did Professor Snape meet with Quirrell so they wouldn't be overheard?

603. What was James Potter's nickname for Snape?

604. Name the potion that Professor Snape threatens to use on Harry?

605. Where does Professor Snape live?

606. What did Mrs Malfoy want Snape to make?

607. What is the name of Snape's mother?

608. ...and his father?

609. Who went to visit Snape in his home?

610. Who does Snape make a monthly potion for whilst he is at Hogwarts?

Creatures and Animals - Part 3

611. What kind of creature is Ronan?

612. Which werewolf bit Remus Lupin?

613. The sound of which creature can kill a Basilisk?

614. Which two types of dragon are found in the British Isles?

615. What animal's blood should you feed (with brandy) to a dragon?

616. Which creatures guard the lake in the cave where Harry finds a horcrux with Dumbledore?

617. What is the name of Aunt Marge's dog?

618. How many giants does Hagrid think there are left?

619. ...and who is the Gurg?

620. What is the name of Hepzibah Smith's house elf?

Spells - Part 4

What would you say if you wanted to cast the following spells?

621. Clears a target's airway if it is blocked.

622. Creates a bandage and a splint.

623. Creates a duplicate of any object.

624. Makes a blindfold appear over a target's eyes.

625. Heals minor injuries.

626. Makes the target vanish.

627. Makes an enlarged object the correct size again.

628. Brings the target back to consciousness if they have been unconscious.

629. Conjures a serpent from the caster's wand.

630. Cleans a target object.

The Lovegoods

631. What is the name of the magazine that Xenophilius publishes?

632. When we are first introduced to Luna, what is her necklace made of?

633. How old was Luna when her mother died?

634. Near which village do the Lovegoods live?

635. In which Hogwarts house is Luna in?

636. Where did Luna and her father go on a holiday paid for by selling an interview with Harry to the *Daily Prophet*?

637. Who does Luna briefly replace as quidditch commentator?

638. Name three creatures Luna believes in which other wizards generally don't.

639. What shape is the doorknocker of the Lovegoods' house?

640. Which animal head does Luna wear whilst watching quidditch?

641. What does Ron vomit after casting a spell with his broken wand?

642. ...and what bit of 'specialist equipment' is given to him to help recover?

643. What are George and Fred's fireworks called?

644. What present did Fred and George try to send to Harry when he was in the hospital wing?

645. What did Bill develop a liking for after being bitten by a werewolf?

646. Which Ministry department does Percy Weasley first work for?

647. What is the name of Percy's girlfriend?

648. Who accompanies Percy to the Weasley's house on Christmas Day?

649. Who provided the twins with venomous tentacula seeds?

650. Who is Mrs Weasley's favourite singer?

Anagrams - Part 2

These are the names of Harry Potter characters, but the letters are jumbled up. Can you unscramble them?

651. Tabloid Bath Hags

652. Airbag Butchery

653. Nerdy Oven Slur

654. For Dicing Dry Frog

655. Cleared Our Flu

656. Label Extra Ringlets

657. Celery Novice

658. Yanks On Parsnip

659. Smug Fur Couriers

660. Lazy Harness Trail

661. Who were Sirius Black's parents?

662. Who is linked to both Hogwarts staff and the hospital?

663. What did Apollyon Pringle do at Hogwarts when Mrs Weasley was a student there?

664. Who were the first two death eaters to make it to the top of the astronomy tower after Draco?

665. Who liked being burned at the stake so much she allowed it to happen forty-seven times?

666. Who does Harry ask the minister to release from prison?

667. What is Neville's great uncle called?

668. What is Mrs Figg's first name?

669. Whose father was an auror called Frank?

670. Who is Sirius's great-great-grandfather?

Harry – Part 5

671. Who tied Harry to a gravestone?

672. What extra subject did Harry take with Snape?

673. From which wood was Harry's mother's wand made from?

674. Which three major items did Harry inherit from Sirius?

675. Who did Harry take to Slughorn's party?

676. Which street does Harry end up in the first time he travels by floo powder?

677. Who did Harry duel with at the "duelling club"?

678. Which ghost did Harry meet when he was in the lake?

679. What was the name of the road on which Harry first saw the knight bus?

680. ...and when he gets on, what name does Harry give Stan instead of his own?

681. What potion would Madam Pomfrey use to help cure colds?

682. What is it called when you leave half of yourself behind when apparating?

683. What potion do Asphodel & Wormwood make?

684. What colour hue does the Dogbreath potion have?

685. What is the name of the world's strongest love potion?

686. What spell does Harry use to dangle Ron by his ankles?

687. What are the three things to think of when casting the apparition spell?

688. What spell is used to put out the fire at Hagrid's?

689. What ancient language do many spells rely on?

690. Which spell would you use to damage an opponent's eyesight?

691. What was His middle name when he was a student at Hogwarts?

692. What is the name given to His inner circle of Followers?

693. What is the name of His pet snake?

694. What was the name of the orphanage He grew up in?

695. In which village did His father live?

696. What type of wood is the wand that He takes off Lucius Malfoy in order to kill Harry made of?

697. What was His mother's maiden name?

698. After graduating from Hogwarts, He worked where for a short amount of time?

699. What are the names of the two children He took into a cave during his time at the orphanage?

700. Recite the verse Peter Pettigrew chants to 'resurrect' Him in Godric's Hollow.

701. Where is the nearest portkey to the Weasleys' home?

702. Who is appointed as Buckbeak's executioner?

703. How much did the Dursleys once give to Harry for his Christmas present?

704. How many Valentine's Day cards did Gilderoy Lockhart say he had received?

705. What length of parchment did Professor Binns ask for on the medieval assembly of European wizards?

706. Which member of the order is a metamorphmagus?

707. Who was caught smuggling flying carpets into Britain?

708. When did The Gryffindor Ghost die?

709. How many people could travel on Barty Crouch's Grandfather's Magic Carpet?

710. What are the four types of dragon used in the Triwizard Tournament?

711. What profession does Ron take up when he leaves Hogwarts?

712. Fred and George once turned Ron's teddy bear into what?

713. When Ron is about five years old his brothers, Fred and George, try and get him to perform what ritual?

714. After Percy graduated from Hogwarts he went to work for the Ministry of Magic in which department?

715. Name Ron's favourite Quidditch team.

716. Name the object Ron inherited from Dumbledore when he died.

717. What does the horcrux show Ron before he destroys it?

718. In *The Half Blood Prince,* Ron is poisoned by mead – but who is it intended for?

719. Ron is godfather to which of Harry's children?

720. Once Bill and Fleur were married they went on to have three children; what were their names?

721. What item does Lord Voldemort order Draco Malfoy to purchase from Borgin and Burkes?

722. Who is it intended for, and who ends up with it?

723. Just after Harry received his first broomstick at Hogwarts, Ron mocked Draco's. What make was it?

724. Who does Draco marry at the end of the Deathly Hallows?

725. ...and who is her older sister?

726. The two have one child together, what do they name it?

727. Which school would Draco have attended had it not been for his mother not wanting him so far away from home?

728. What is English translation of the motto written on the Malfoy crest?

729. What was the name of Lucius's father?

730. What were the names of Narcissa's parents?

Can you name the creature being described?

731. A cross between a manticore and a firecrab.

732. Muggles call this flightless bird the dodo.

733. Serves as a guardian for a tree whose wood is used for making wands.

734. Crab-like parasite commonly found in the fur and feathers of crups and augureys.

735. Elfish creature which uses its high-pitched cackle to lure children away from their guardians so it can eat them.

736. Small golden bird used in early games of Quidditch before the invention of the snitch.

737. Furry spherical creature which makes a lovely pet – it emits a humming sound when content.

738. Atlantic ocean fish which seeks out and destroys muggle fishing nets.

739. Small blue speckled bird – silent until it is about to die.

740. Five-legged beast also known as a Hairy MacBoon.

Spells - Part 5

What do these spells do?

741. Cave Inimicum

742. Repello Muggletum

743. Confringo

744. Deletrius

745. Orchideous

746. Langlock

747. Specialis Revelio

748. Mobiliarbus

749. Waddiwasi

750. Colloportus

Who Plays - Part 4

In the films, who plays these characters?

751. Aunt Petunia Dursley

752. Dudley Dursley

753. Mr. Ollivander

754. Percy Weasley

755. Seamus Finnigan

756. Lee Jordan

757. Argus Filch

758. Moaning Myrtle

759. Professor Lupin

760. Viktor Krum

761. Who was the last Gryffindor seeker to help win the quidditch cup?

762. What position did Lockhart say he played at quidditch?

763. How many seconds does it take a Firebolt to accelerate from zero to 150 miles per hour?

764. What quidditch team does Cho Chang support?

765. Who does Oliver Wood play for after leaving Hogwarts?

766. So who takes over from him at Gryffindor?

767. Who captains the Holyhead Harpies?

768. How many years had it been since Britain last hosted the quidditch World Cup?

769. What colour was the dark mark skull in the sky when Britain did host it after all that time?

770. ...and which house elf did Harry meet there?

771. Name two of the four girls Hermione shares a dormitory with.

772. In The Philosopher's (or Sorcerer's) stone, what spell does Hermione conjure to free the trio from the Devil's Snare?

773. What did Hermione transfigure a match into during her first class with Professor McGonagall?

774. Name one of the two things Hermione smells in the Love Potion.

775. With whom does Hermione attend Professor Slughorn's Christmas party?

776. What method of flying did Hermione use in the battle of the seven Potters?

777. ...and who accompanied her?

778. Hermione used polyjuice potion to infiltrate the Ministry of Magic – but who does she turn into?

779. What magical plant does Hermione use to heal Harry's bite from Nagini?

780. Describe Hermione's wand.

781. What is Albus Dumbledore's full name?

782. What is his Animagus form?

783. Before becoming headmaster at Hogwarts, Dumbledore taught which lesson?

784. Dumbledore is incredibly well known throughout the wizarding world, but the defeat of which wizard added to this fame?

785. When Dumbledore looks into the mirror of Erised, his deepest, most desperate desires are revealed to him, but what does he tell Harry he sees?

786. What are the names of Dumbledore's parents?

787. Where did the Dumbledore family live before they moved to Godric's Hollow?

788. Dumbledore's mother died in a terrible accident caused by whom?

789. Dumbledore is removed as chief warlock of the Wizengamot, but he says he doesn't care as long as they don't eliminate him from something else – what is it?

790. What are the 'few words' that Dumbledore says at the feast at the start of Harry's first year?

791. In *The Chamber of Secrets*, Dobby visits Harry and Harry asks him to do something a wizard has never asked him to do before. What is it?

792. When Harry infiltrated the Ministry, who was he disguised as?

793. What extra subject did Harry take with Snape?

794. Which vault in Gringotts belongs to the Potter Family?

795. When Ron is poisoned in The Half Blood Prince, what does Harry feed to him?

796. In *The Prisoner of Azkaban,* Harry is sat in the Leaky Cauldron watching what looks to be a hag in a woollen balaclava who orders a plate of what?

797. In *The Philosopher's Stone,* Harry is sat in the great hall when he receives a long, thin parcel via screech owl – knocking which item of his food onto the floor?

798. Harry ends up having three children; what are their names?

799. What does Hermione use to cure Harry's bite from Nagini?

800. Over which city was the baby Harry Potter flying in Hagrid's motorbike when he fell asleep?

The Answers

Harry - Part 1

1. 31st July

2. 4 Privet Drive, Little Whinging

3. Hagrid

4. A Lightning Bolt

5. A Boa-Constrictor

6. James

7. Lily

8. An Invisibility Cloak

9. A Stag

10. Cho Chang

Spells – Part 1

11. Repairs broken or damaged objects.

12. A Summoning charm.

13. Causes an object to swell in size.

14. Disarms another wizard.

15. Used to fight a boggart.

16. Produces fire.

17. Creates a beam of light.

18. Magnifies the spellcaster's voice.

19. Causes the target to become confused.

20. Prevents nearby people from hearing a conversation.

Hermione - Part 1

21. Jean

22. An Otter

23. Viktor Krum

24. Gryffindor

25. Crookshanks

26. It made her teeth grow

27. Defence Against The Dark Arts

28. Full Body Bind

29. Dentists

30. September

Who Plays - Part 1

31. Daniel Radcliffe

32. Robbie Coltrane

33. Richard Griffiths

34. Bonnie Wright

35. Rupert Grint

36. Emma Watson

37. Tom Felton

38. John Cleese

39. Alan Rickman

40. Gary Oldman

Ron - Part 1

41. Ginger

42. Bilius

43. Six

44. A Howler

45. A Pocket Sneakoscope

46. Spellotape

47. A Knight

48. True

49. A Spider

50. Keeper

Gryffindors

51. Lavender Brown

52. A milkman

53. Beater

54. A fox

55. Fred Weasley

56. Trevor

57. He had eaten poisonous doxy eggs as a bet.

58. Romilda Vane

59. Lee Jordan

60. Instructions that he would be doing his detention no matter how many party invitations he had received.

Hogwarts – Part 1

61. Never tickle a sleeping dragon

62. The Sorting Hat

63. Green

64. A Poltergeist

65. Thestrals

66. Caput Draconis

67. Badger, Eagle, Lion and Snake

68. Hannah Abbott

69. 437

70. Pinefresh

71. Mrs Norris

72. Firenze

73. Skele-gro

74. Quirinus Quirrell

75. Professor Sinistra

76. The Half-Blood Prince, Snivellus, Snivelly, Sev or Slytherus Snape.

77. Hufflepuff

78. Dolores Umbridge

79. Charity Burbage

80. Professor Grubbly-Plank

The Wizarding World - Part 1

Fantastic Beasts - Part 1

91. Acromantula

92. Centaur

93. Doxy

94. Flobberworm

95. Hippogriff

96. Kneazle

97. Leprechaun

98. Nargle

99. Phoenix

100. Thestral

Creatures and Animals - Part 1

101. The Philosophers Stone

102. Music (specifically a Harp)

103. Trevor

104. Errol

105. Buckbeak

106. Witherwings

107. A Boarhound

108. Basilisk

109. The Unicorn

110. 4

Dumbledore and Family - Part 1

121. Padfoot

122. Thirteen

123. Bellatrix Lestrange

124. His cousin

125. He used his animagus form, as dementors were less able to detect animals.

126. The enchanted motorbike

127. 12 Grimmauld Place

128. Kreacher

129. Regulus

130. Snuffles

Quidditch - Part 1

131. Bludger, Quaffle and Golden Snitch

132. 150

133. 7

134. Beater, Chaser, Keeper and Seeker

135. Chudley Cannons

136. A Nimbus 2000

137. Oliver Wood

138. Dobby

139. Marcus Flint

140. 700

The Malfoys and Friends - Part 1

Spells – Part 2

151. Avada Kedavra

152. Alohomora

153. Portus

154. Silencio

155. Expecto Patronum

156. Crucio

157. Stupefy

158. Prior Incantato

159. Obliviate

160. Morsmordre

Harry – Part 2

161. On his forehead

162. His mother, father, Sirius and of course Harry himself.

163. Slytherin

164. James

165. Eleventh

166. The Killing Curse (Avada Kedavra)

167. A Nimbus 2000

168. Vernon and Petunia Dursley

169. Ginny Weasley

170. A car crash

Patronuses

171. A Stag

172. A Jack Russell

173. A Horse

174. A Phoenix

175. A Lynx

176. A Hare

177. A Doe

178. A Cat

179. A Swan

180. A Goat

181. Parseltongue

182. You can assume the form of an animal

183. The Wiggenweld Potion

184. A Demiguise

185. The hair becomes more opaque and therefore the cloak loses its effectiveness

186. The ability to read others' minds

187. The ability to close one's mind to a Legilimens

188. Wolfsbane

189. Mandragora

190. It increases your brain power

The Weasleys - Part 1

191. Ronald Bilius Weasley

192. A spider

193. Bill, Charlie, Percy, Fred, George and Ginny

194. Fred

195. One of the Weasley's family owls

196. The Chamber of Secrets

197. Scabbers

198. Romania

199. A Werewolf

200. A Ford Anglia

Other Characters - Part 1

201. Professor Albus Dumbledore

202. Death Eaters

203. Madam Rosmerta

204. Stan Shunpike

205. Ernie Prang

206. Nicolas Flamel

207. Lee Jordan

208. Dennis

209. Regulus

210. Cedric Diggory

211. He killed himself with the same knife he used to kill Helena Ravenclaw when he couldn't get her to return from Albania.

212. Millicent Bulstrode

213. Both are beaters.

214. Fiendfyre

215. Eight – he had to repeat his last year because he failed his exams.

216. Pansy Parkinson

217. Blaise Zabini

218. Theodore Nott

219. Graham Montague

220. Terence Higgs

Books and the Like - Part 1

221. Red

222. The Daily Prophet

223. Hogwarts: A History

224. Chroniclus Punnet

225. Stroke its Spine

226. Which Broomstick

227. The Quibbler

228. Most Charming Smile

229. Bathilda Bagshot

230. The Half Blood Prince

The Weasleys - Part 2

Ravenclaws

241. Cho Chang

242. Marcus Belby

243. Baruffio's Brain Elixir

244. Penelope Clearwater

245. Moaning Myrtle

246. Padma

247. The Grey Lady

248. Professor Flitwick

249. Roger Davies

250. Michael Corner

Hogwarts Staff - Part 2

251. Professor Flitwick

252. Professor McGonagall

253. 39 years

254. A Tabby Cat

255. Professor Binns

256. He is a Werewolf

257. Pomona

258. Professor Dippet

259. Professor Kettleburn

260. He is a Squib

261. Devil's Snare

262. Mermish

263. Stonewall High

264. He transformed into a Dog

265. Snuffles

266. Your Soul

267. Professor Umbridge

268. The Malfoys

269. Purple

270. Devon

Teachers and Their Subjects

281. They were intercepted by Dobby

282. The piano

283. Hector Dagworth-Granger

284. On the Hogwarts Express

285. A basilisk

286. Mudblood

287. A time-turner

288. The Ministry of Magic

289. The Sixth

290. Professor McGonagall telling her that she had failed everything.

Shops

291. Ollivander's

292. Seven

293. Florean Fortescue

294. The Hogs Head and the Three Broomsticks

295. Weasleys Wizard Wheezes

296. 93 Diagon Alley

297. Robes

298. Honeydukes

299. The Magical Menagerie

300. Twelve Galleons

301. Lord Voldemort

302. Nagini

303. False

304. None

305. Thirteen and a half inches

306. The Hogwarts assistance fund

307. Borgin and Burke's

308. Ten Galleons

309. They are both Half-Bloods, they are both Orphans, and they both speak Parseltongue.

310. Little Hangleton

Hagrid

321. The Malfoys

322. He ironed them.

323. One Galleon

324. Aberforth Dumbledore's

325. In the gardens of Shell Cottage

326. A bludger

327. Winky

328. He used it to hide Winky in when she was drunk.

329. Harry's Wheezy

330. "Harry... Potter."

Ron - Part 2

341. Colin Creevey

342. One year and three months

343. The Grim

344. Moaning Myrtle

345. Brazil

346. Basketball

347. St Brutus' Secure Centre for Incurably Criminal Boys

348. A Hungarian Horntail

349. Phoenix feather

350. The snitch from Harry's first ever game of Quidditch.

Hogwarts - Part 2

Who Said?

361. Dumbledore

362. Hagrid

363. Ron

364. Percy Weasley

365. Kingsley Shacklebolt

366. Hermione

367. Draco

368. Tom Riddle

369. Harry

370. Sirius

Creatures and Animals - Part 2

371. A Troll

372. A Snowy Owl

373. An Acromantula

374. Hagrid, Harry and Professor Slughorn

375. Acromantula Venom

376. The Kitchens at Hogwarts

377. Firenze

378. A Dog

379. Kreacher

380. A Spider

381. Cho Chang

382. Seamus Finnegan

383. Peru

384. Bulgaria

385. Ireland

386. Hassan Mostafa

387. 10 Galleons

388. Mahogany

389. Professor Umbridge

390. A Firebolt

Who Plays - Part 2

391. Maggie Smith

392. Ian Hart

393. Julie Walters

394. James & Oliver Phelps

395. Matthew Lewis

396. Jamie Waylett

397. Josh Herdman

398. Zoë Wanamaker

399. Jason Isaacs

400. Kenneth Branagh

401. Hermione took the blame away from them after they were attacked by a troll.

402. S.P.E.W.

403. Winky – and by Bartemius Crouch.

404. Rose and Hugo

405. Ravenclaw

406. Because brainy students are usually sorted there!

407. Millicent Bulstrode

408. An Otter

409. The Tales of Beedle the Bard

410. The Protean charm

Hufflepuffs

411. Cedric Diggory

412. Hannah Abbott

413. Professor Sprout

414. Susan Bones

415. Justin Finch-Fletchley

416. Ernie Macmillan

417. The Fat Friar

418. Zacharias Smith

419. Summerby – we're not told his first name.

420. Cadwallader – again, we don't know his first name!

421. The Elixir of Life

422. Polyjuice Potion

423. To cure those who have been Petrified

424. Wolfsbane

425. Liquid Luck

426. Six Months

427. Gillyweed

428. They tell the truth

429. Bubotuber

430. Thick, black and slug-like

Anagrams - Part 1

431. Harry Potter

432. Sirius Black

433. Draco Malfoy

434. Luna Lovegood

435. Albus Dumbledore

436. Ron Weasley

437. Seamus Finney

438. Hermione Granger

439. Rubeus Hagrid

440. Neville Longbottom

441. Sitting in front of the staff-room fire

442. Professor Flitwick

443. Rolanda

444. Professor Kettleburn

445. Lilac

446. A Grindylow

447. Piertotum Locomotor

448. Budleigh Babberton

449. That they should be rounded up and tagged

450. Apollyon Pringle

Other Characters - Part 2

461. The Deathstick and the Wand of Destiny

462. True

463. Avada Kedavra, Crucio and Imperio

464. Albus Dumbledore

465. Felix Felicis

466. The 7th

467. A gargoyle

468. Stanley Shunpike

469. Grawp

470. 0-150mph in 10 seconds

471. Produces a jet of water from the caster's wand.

472. Ties the target up with ropes.

473. Makes the steps of a stairway flatten and form a slide.

474. Makes a target dance uncontrollably.

475. Cuts or rips an object.

476. Avis Oppugno

477. Homenum Revelio

478. Densaugeo

479. Rictusempra

480. Descendo

The Weasleys - Part 3

481. The Marauder's Map

482. Mollywobbles

483. Fifty

484. Onion Soup

485. Barty Crouch

486. Weatherby

487. Twelve

488. Hermes

489. The Misuse of Muggle Artefacts Office

490. One

The Dursleys

491. Grunnings

492. Thirty-Six

493. Big D

494. Dudders

495. St. Brutus's Secure Centre for Incurably Criminal Boys

496. Twelve

497. The Accidental Magic Reversal Department

498. Red

499. Uncle Vernon

500. The Rail View Hotel

Hogwarts Staff - Part 4

501. Filius

502. An Examiner

503. Horace Slughorn

504. Hagrid

505. Firenze

506. Poppy

507. Gilderoy Lockhart

508. Professor Sprout

509. Astronomy

510. Professors Dumbledore and McGonagall

511. Nastily Exhausting Wizarding Tests

512. The Shrieking Shack

513. Neville Longbottom

514. Remus Lupin, Peter Pettigrew, Sirius Black and James Potter

515. Kingsley Shacklebolt

516. Buckbeak

517. Fleur Delacour

518. 713

519. Sir Nicholas de Mimsy-Porpington

520. Forty-five

The Malfoys and Friends - Part 2

521. Gregory

522. A wounded unicorn

523. Moaning Myrtle

524. Charity Burbage

525. Unicorn hair

526. Lucius and Narcissa

527. True

528. Black

529. Hippogriff

530. A ferret

531. The Tales of Beedle the Bard

532. Seven Hundred

533. A Belt

534. Roonil Wazlib

535. Libatius Borage

536. Eldred Worple

537. In Limericks

538. Common Magical Ailments and Afflictions

539. Vindictus Viridian

540. Inigo Imago

541. By agreement from both captains

542. Ten

543. 150

544. False – it is every *four* years

545. Hitting bludgers towards spectators

546. The final of the 1473 World cup

547. The Gimbi Giant-Slayers, the Patonga Proudsticks, the Sumbawanga Sunrays or the Tchamba Charmers

548. False – players can take their wands onto the pitch, but they must not be used on or against any players, any players' broomsticks, the referee, any of the four balls, or the spectators!

549. The Tarapoto Tree-Skimmers

550. Kennilworthy Whisp

Harry - Part 4

Dumbledore and Family - Part 2

561. It was a password to his office

562. Gryffindor

563. It is a good oven cleaner

564. Minister of Magic

565. Professor Snape

566. Aberforth

567. Ariana

568. His father, Percival

569. The Hog's Head Inn

570. Auburn

571. Hugh Mitchell

572. Mark Williams

573. Emma Thompson

574. Timothy Spall

575. David Tennant

576. Robert Pattinson

577. Katie Leung

578. Clemence Poesy

579. Ralph Fiennes

580. Bill Nighy

581. (The) Society for the Promotion of Elfish Welfare

582. Two Sickles

583. Hats and Socks for the House Elves

584. Dumbledore's Army

585. A Fake Galleon

586. Confundus

587. Cormac McLaggen

588. Professor Slughorn's

589. Charms

590. Ron

The Wizarding World - Part 2

Professor Snape

601. Defence Against the Dark Arts Teacher

602. The Forbidden Forest

603. Snivellus

604. Veritaserum

605. Spinner's End

606. An Unbreakable Vow

607. Eileen Prince

608. Tobias Snape

609. Bellatrix Lestrange and Narcissa Malfoy

610. Professor Lupin

Creatures and Animals - Part 3

611. A Centaur

612. Fenrir Greyback

613. A Rooster

614. The Common Welsh Green and The Hebridean Black

615. Chicken

616. Inferi

617. Ripper

618. Eighty

619. The Chief of the Giants

620. Hokey

621. Anapneo

622. Ferula

623. Geminio

624. Obscuro

625. Episkey

626. Evanesco

627. Reducio

628. Rennervate

629. Serpensortia

630. Scourgify

The Lovegoods

631. The Quibbler

632. Butterbeer caps

633. Nine

634. Ottery St. Catchpole

635. Ravenclaw

636. Sweden

637. Zacharias Smith

638. Any of the following: moon frogs, blibbering humdingers, crumple-horned snorkacks, heliopaths, umgubular slashkilters, nargles, aquavirius maggots, wrackspurts, gulping plimpies and dabberblimps.

639. An eagle

640. A lion

641. Slugs

642. A Bucket

643. Weasleys' Wildfire Whiz-Bangs

644. A Toilet Seat

645. Rare Steak

646. The Department of International Magical Co-operation

647. Penelope Clearwater

648. Rufus Scrimgeour

649. Mundungus Fletcher

650. Celestina Warbeck

Anagrams - Part 2

651. Bathilda Bagshot

652. Charity Burbage

653. Vernon Dursley

654. Godric Gryffindor

655. Fleur Delacour

656. Bellatrix Lestrange

657. Colin Creevey

658. Pansy Parkinson

659. Rufus Scrimgeour

660. Salazar Slytherin

Other Characters - Part 3

661. Orion and Walburga

662. Dilys Derwent

663. He was the caretaker

664. Alecto and Amycus

665. Wendelin the Weird

666. Stan Shunpike

667. Algie

668. Arabella

669. Neville Longbottom

670. Phineas Nigellus

Harry - Part 5

691. Marvolo

692. Death Eaters

693. Nagini

694. Wool's Orphanage

695. Little Hangleton

696. Elm

697. Gaunt

698. Borgin and Burkes

699. Dennis Bishop and Amy Benson

700. "Bone of the father, unknowingly given, you will renew your son. Flesh of the servant, willingly sacrificed, you will revive your master. Blood of the enemy, forcibly taken, you will resurrect your foe."

701. Stoatshead Hill

702. Walden MacNair

703. Fifty Pence

704. Forty-six

705. Three Feet

706. Nymphadora Tonks

707. Ali Bashir

708. The 31st October 1492

709. Twelve

710. The Chinese Fireball, The Hungarian Horntail, The Swedish Short-Snout and The Welsh Green

The Weasleys - Part 5

711. An auror

712. A spider

713. An unbreakable vow

714. The Department of International Magical Cooperation

715. Chudley Cannons

716. A deluminator

717. Harry and Hermione kissing

718. Dumbledore

719. James

720. Victoire, Dominique and Louis

The Malfoys and Friends - Part 3

721. An opal necklace

722. Dumbledore and Katy Bell

723. A Comet 260

724. Astoria Greengrass

725. Daphne Greengrass

726. Scorpius Hyperion Malfoy

727. Durmstrang

728. Purity will always conquer

729. Abraxas Malfoy

730. Cygnus and Druella

Fantastic Beasts - Part 2

731. Blast-Ended Skrewt

732. Diricawl

733. Bowtruckle

734. Chizpurfle

735. Erkling

736. Golden Snidget

737. Puffskein

738. Shrake

739. Jobberknoll

740. Quintaped

741. Strengthens an enclosure from enemies.

742. Keeps Muggles away from wizarding places.

743. Makes the target explode into flames.

744. Removes evidence of previous spells cast by a wand.

745. Makes flowers appear out of the caster's wand.

746. Glues the victim's tongue to the roof of their mouth.

747. Makes an object reveal its magical properties.

748. Lifts a tree slightly off the ground allowing it to be moved.

749. Launches small objects through the air.

750. Magically locks a door.

Who Plays - Part 4

751. Fiona Shaw

752. Harry Melling

753. John Hurt

754. Chris Rankin

755. Devon Murray

756. Luke Youngblood

757. David Bradley

758. Shirley Henderson

759. David Thewlis

760. Stanislav Ianevski

761. Charlie Weasley

762. Seeker

763. Ten

764. The Tutshill Tornados

765. Puddlemere United

766. Angelina Johnson

767. Gwenog Jones

768. Thirty Years

769. Emerald Green

770. Winky

771. Lavender Brown, Parvati Patil and Fay Dunbar – the fourth girl (who we're told is friends with Fay) is never named.

772. Lumos Solem

773. Needle

774. Freshly mowed grass and new parchment

775. Cormac McLaggen

776. A Thestral

777. Kingsley Shacklebolt

778. Mafalda Hopkirk

779. Dittany

780. Ten and three quarter inch vine wood wand with a dragon heartstring core

781. Albus Percival Wulfric Brian Dumbledore

782. A swan

783. Transfiguration

784. Gellert Grindelwald

785. Himself holding a pair of thick woollen socks.

786. Percival and Kendra

787. Mould-on-the-Wold

788. Ariana, his sister

789. Chocolate frog cards

790. Nitwit, blubber, oddment and tweak

Harry – Part 6

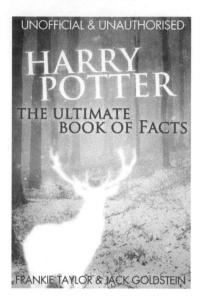

Are you a huge fan of Harry Potter? You have probably read every book and seen every film many times over. But how much do you really know? This excellent book has more than two hundred facts that will surprise and amaze you in equal measure. Sections include:

- Harry Potter and Daniel Radcliffe
- Quidditch
- Hermione Granger and Emma Watson
- The Ministry of Magic
- The Triwizard Tournament
- Hogwarts
- And many more

If you love Harry Potter and want to expand your knowledge of the series, this is the perfect way to do it!